Jewelry School
Let's Start Beading

Dedication

I would like to dedicate this book to Louise Thurston, who believed in me enough to hire me to teach at West Herts College. Her support and encouragement played a major role in my development as a teacher both in the classroom and through books and various other media.

First published in Great Britain 2016

Search Press Limited
Wellwood, North Farm Road,
Tunbridge Wells, Kent TN2 3DR

Text copyright © Carolyn Schulz 2016

Photographs by Paul Bricknell at Search Press Studios

Photographs and design copyright © Search Press Ltd. 2016

ISBN: 978-1-78221-258-4

The Publishers and author can accept no responsibility for any consequences arising from the information, advice or instructions given in this publication.

Publishers' note
You are invited to visit the author's website at www.carolynschulz.com

Suppliers
If you have difficulty in obtaining any of the materials and equipment mentioned in this book, then please visit the Search Press website for details of suppliers: www.searchpress.com

Printed in China

Acknowledgements

I must firstly thank the team at Search Press for their patience and support, particularly Sophie Kersey for editorial support, Paul Bricknell for the gorgeous photography and Marrianne Miall for designing an absolutely wonderful book that is clear, perfect for beginners and beyond what I envisaged.

A special mention also goes to Beadalon (www.beadalon.com) for supplying their top quality tools and components which I always use and recommend to my students due to their unrivalled quality, and to Solid Oak (www.solidoakllc.com) for also supplying materials and especially for creating amazing kits that correspond with the techniques featured in the book.

Last but not least, thank you to everyone who has purchased a copy of this book. It is my sincere hope that it will create and inspire a whole new generation of jewellery makers!

Jewelry School
Let's Start Beading

Carolyn Schulz

SEARCH PRESS

Contents

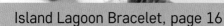

STRETCHY CORD 44

Glitter Ball Ring, page 46

Seashore Crystal
Cha-Cha Ring, page 50

Seashore Crystal
Cha-Cha Bracelet, page 54

CHAIN & JUMP RINGS 56

Sweetheart Charm Bracelet,
page 62

Two-on-two Chain Maille
Bracelet, page 66

Shaggy Loop Chain Maille
Bracelet, page 70

Introduction

Creativity has been an important part of my life, with my mother and both grandmothers sharing their love of sewing, knitting and crafting with me from an early age. Living the ex-pat life until my teens provided both the need and opportunity to make all those things from home that weren't available in the countries where we resided. But it wasn't until my thirties that I was introduced to beads and creating fashion jewellery.

From my first introduction to making jewellery at a craft show 'make and take', I was hooked. Despite searching all over for a beginners' course, all I could find were individual classes offered here and there. So with the help of classes, kits, books, magazines and personal tuition from experts, I set about soaking up everything that I could about working with beads and making jewellery.

The melding together of my two loves, making and designing jewellery with teaching finally came eight years ago when I was offered the opportunity to develop and teach Beginners' Creative Jewellery at West Herts College.

This book is the culmination of the course I developed based on my own experience. It uses simple basic techniques and affordable beads and components to make gorgeous fashionable jewellery. And the best thing about it is that you don't need to be a crafter already – anyone can make jewellery!

MEMORY WIRE

Memory wire is hardened steel wire which, because of its hard temper, holds its shape.

It can be either round or flat.

It comes in ring, bracelet and necklace sizes. Bracelet memory wire also comes in an oval shape to imitate the shape of the wrist, and in small, regular and large.

Memory wire is very stiff and you will need to use strength when forming loops at the ends.

Memory wire coils may loosen depending on the shape and weight of the beads you use.

Memory wire is particularly good for those who find fiddling with clasps a challenge.

Tips for use

- Memory wire should never be cut using jewellery grade wire cutters; always use memory wire shears.
- Memory wire ends can be looped to prevent beads from slipping off or have half-drilled beads or purpose-made endings glued over them.
- Small seed beads or E-beads between larger beads will cover wire exposed by the curving shape.
- Generally, use a minimum of three coils of memory wire as fewer can result in the bracelet losing its shape.
- When using bracelet memory wire, use the larger size if you are using large or heavy beads.

TOOLS

Memory wire shears

Memory wire finishing pliers

Round-nosed pliers

Chain-nosed pliers

Flush cutters

BIRTHSTONE BRACELET

Because of its versatility, memory wire continues to gain popularity with jewellery makers. Whether it is a basic coiled bracelet or a sophisticated cuff, the results are satisfying to make and stylish to wear. They make great gifts, especially when personalised, like these quick and easy birthstone bracelets. I have used pink beads to represent pink tourmaline, the birthstone for October, but you can choose whatever is appropriate for your bracelet (see the birthstones chart below).

MATERIALS
99 (approx.) 4mm glass ivory pearls
3 4mm AB crystal faceted bicone beads
1 4mm pink faceted bicone bead
5 6mm AB crystal faceted bicone beads
17 6mm pink faceted bicone beads
4 8mm AB crystal faceted bicone beads
22 11/0 (small) silver seed beads
3½ coils of silver memory wire
4 silver-plated ball-end headpins

What you learn
- How to make a P-shaped loop to keep the beads in place
- How to make a wrapped loop to create dangles
- How to create coiled memory wire pieces

Birthstones

January: Garnet
February: Amethyst
March: Aquamarine
April: Diamond
May: Emerald
June: Smoky quartz

July: Ruby
August: Peridot
September: Sapphire
October: Pink tourmaline
November: Citrine
December: Blue topaz

The dangles made for the ends of this coiled memory wire bracelet can also be used to make earrings. All you need to do is attach them to the loop at the end of an earring wire or earring post.

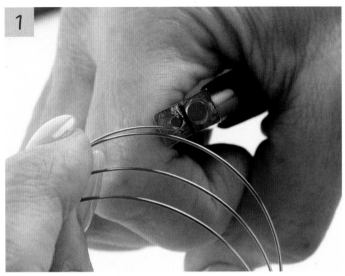

1 Use memory wire shears to cut three and a half coils of bracelet size memory wire. Using memory wire finishing pliers (or round-nosed pliers), make a P-shaped loop at one end of the wire so that the loop curls out and away from the coils of wire.

2 At the other end of the wire, thread on one small silver seed bead, one 4mm AB crystal faceted bicone and a second small silver seed bead. Follow by threading 4mm glass ivory pearls (about forty-five, depending on the size of memory wire coils) until one full coil is filled. For smaller diameter memory wire, you will overlap into the second coil, which will stretch out when worn. Finish with a small silver seed bead, a 4mm glass ivory pearl and a small silver seed bead. Push the beads around all the coils until they are next to the P-shaped loop from step 1.

Tips

- I prefer to use the small barrel of the memory wire finishing pliers for a less obvious loop.
- Wire is very stiff so you will need to grip tightly and use real strength to make the loop.

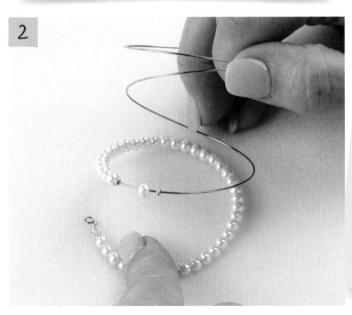

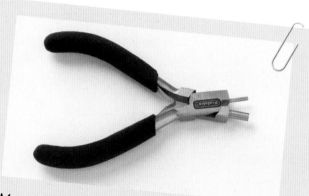

Memory wire finishing pliers

Cone-shaped round-nosed pliers can slip when you are trying to form a loop from the hardened steel of memory wire. Memory wire finishing pliers have one small rod and one large rod, both straight cylinders. This eliminates slippage and makes it easier to form loops of a consistent size.

3 Continue by threading the following pattern four times to fill the second (middle) coil of memory wire:
- 6mm pink faceted bicone
- 6mm AB crystal faceted bicone
- 6mm pink faceted bicone
- Silver seed bead
- 4mm glass ivory pearl
- Silver seed bead
- 6mm pink faceted bicone
- 8mm AB crystal faceted bicone
- 6mm pink faceted bicone
- Silver seed bead
- 4mm glass ivory pearl
- Silver seed bead

4 Thread on the same number of 4mm glass ivory pearls as added in step 2 (about forty-five). Finish with a seed bead, a 4mm AB crystal faceted bicone and a final seed bead.

5 Use memory wire shears to cut the excess wire, leaving approximately 8mm (¾in) or whatever length is needed to form a P-shaped loop to hold all the beads tightly in place.

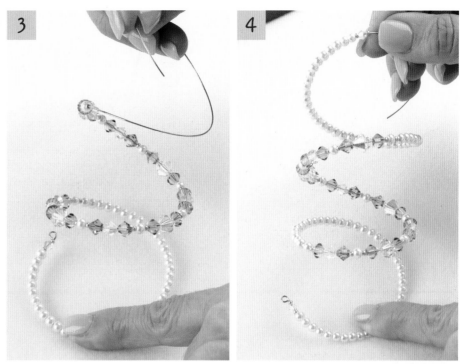

HOW TO MAKE A WRAPPED LOOP

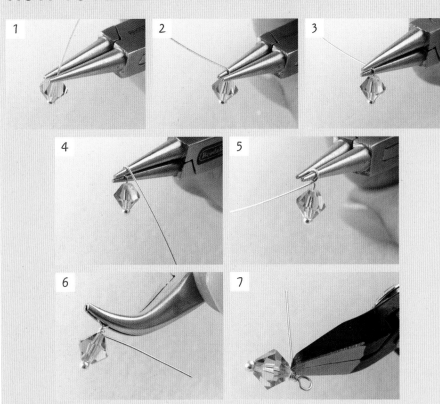

6 Make a dangle with a 6mm pink faceted bicone, using the instructions for making a wrapped loop (left). Make another dangle with a 4mm AB crystal faceted bicone. Hang these from the P-shaped loop at one end of the memory wire. Make a dangle from a 6mm AB crystal faceted bicone and another from a 4mm pink faceted bicone, and hang these from the P-shaped loop at the other end of the bracelet.

1 Using round-nosed pliers, hold the bead on a headpin so that it is tight against the head.

2 Bend the wire at right angles with your finger. The round-nosed pliers should be horizontal as shown.

3 Shift the barrels of the round-nosed pliers so they are vertical.

4 Use your fingers to pull the wire tight around the top barrel of the pliers, then down. Pull so that the wire is tight around the barrel and down as far as it can go.

5 Shift the barrels again to make them horizontal. Use your fingers to pull the wire around the barrel of the pliers to form a complete loop.

Note

If you are attaching this unit to another component such as P-shaped loop, be sure to attach it now, BEFORE step 6.

6 Change to bent-nosed pliers and hold the loop. Twist the wire two to three times, or as many as required, around the gap between the bead and the loop.

7 Use flush cutters to trim the end of the wire.

Designer Tips

- Use E-beads (larger seed beads), spacer beads, diamante spacers or bead caps to separate and add interest to the design.

- Create a different texture by using seed beads between larger beads.

Design Inspiration

February's birthstone is amethyst while May is represented by emerald. It couldn't be easier to substitute whichever birthstone colour is required to make this gorgeous bracelet for all those special people in your life!

ISLAND LAGOON BRACELET

Use bright greens and brilliant shades of blue shell rondelle to frame natural turquoise nuggets and create a stunning bracelet. A touch of silver between the nuggets separates them and draws attention to the unique beauty of each individual shape.

MATERIALS

250–300 small aqua/green shell rondelles

12 10–12mm turquoise nuggets

32 11/0 (small) silver seed beads

18 6/0 (large) silver seed beads

3½ coils of silver memory wire

2 silver-plated flat headpins

1

1 Use memory wire shears to cut three and a half coils of bracelet size memory wire and with memory wire finishing pliers (or round-nosed pliers) make a P-shaped loop at one end of the wire (see page 12). Thread from the other end: one 11/0 (small) silver seed bead, one 6/0 (large) silver seed bead and a second small silver seed bead. Follow by filling one full coil of memory wire with aqua and green shell rondelles. Push the seed beads and shell rondelles around all the coils until they are next to the P-shaped loop.

Once you have learned how to make dangles like those attached to the ends of this bracelet, you can adapt them to make earrings. Just attach them to the loop at the end of an earring wire, post or clip.

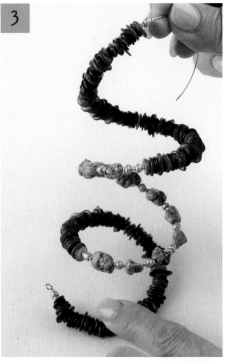

2 Continue by threading the following pattern twelve times or however many times required to fill the second (middle) coil of memory wire:

- 11/0 (small) silver seed bead
- 6/0 (large) silver seed bead
- 11/0 (small) silver seed bead
- 10–12mm turquoise nugget

3 Fill the third coil of wire with aqua and green shell rondelles and finish with one small silver seed bead, one large silver seed bead and a second small silver seed bead as a mirror image to the first coil.

4 Use memory wire shears to cut the excess wire, leaving approximately 8mm (¾in) or whatever length is needed to form a P-shaped loop to hold all the beads tightly in place.

5 Make two dangles, following the instructions for making a wrapped loop (see page 14), each with the following beads:

- 11/0 (small) silver seed bead
- 6/0 (large) silver seed bead
- 4–5 aqua/green shell rondelles
- 6/0 (large) silver seed bead
- 11/0 (small) silver seed bead

Hang one dangle on each P-shaped end loop.

Design inspiration

In contrast to our Island Lagoon Bracelet, what could be more elegant than this five-stranded pearl and crystal bracelet? The middle strand of crystal clusters separated by satin pearls and gold seed beads is framed by two strands of round and oval pearls on either side. The dangles can be duplicated to make elegant earrings, completing an exquisite ensemble.

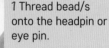

AFTER EIGHT CUFF

This is a simply stunning cuff of white glass pearls and faceted crystals.
I have named it After Eight because it would embellish any 'little black
dress', but with its simple black and white theme, it could be worn at
any time of day, with any colour scheme.

What you learn

- How to make a basic loop on an eye pin or headpin
- How to create cuffs using memory wire

MATERIALS

94 4mm white glass pearls
23 6 x 8mm faceted jet crystal rondelles
42 10/0 silver seed beads
Memory wire
23 silver-plated eye pins
2 silver-plated headpins
4 silver-plated ball-end headpins

1 Cut two coils of memory wire with a
5–10cm (2–4in) overlap. With memory wire
finishing pliers (or round-nosed pliers) make
a P-shaped loop at one end of the wire (see
page 12). Next prepare twenty-one silver-
plated eye pins by threading a silver seed
bead, a faceted jet crystal rondelle and a
second silver seed bead onto each. Proceed
to make a basic loop on each eye pin as
shown right.

MAKING A BASIC LOOP

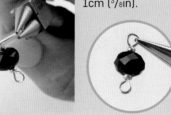

1 Thread bead/s
onto the headpin or
eye pin.

2 With chain-nosed
pliers, bend the
wire extending
above the bead/s
at right angles, as
close to the bead as
possible.

3 Cut off excess
wire, leaving a
small arm of about
1cm (³/₈in).

4 With round-nosed
pliers, grab the very
end of the pin about
6mm (¼in) from
the tip of the pliers.
Twist the wire back
towards where the
wire comes out of
the bead, wrapping
it tightly around a
barrel of the pliers
to make a loop.

The finished loop
should be positioned
centrally over the
holes of the beads.

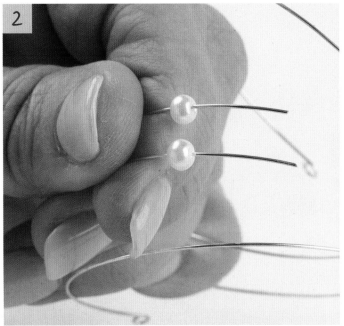

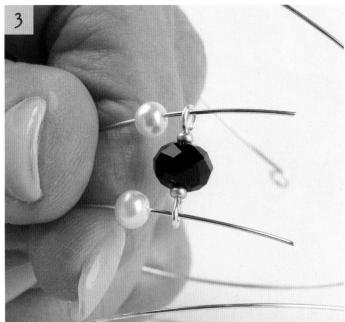

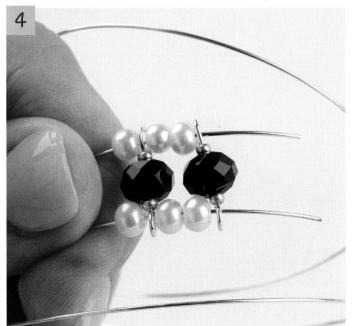

2 Pick up the two pieces of memory wire and hold together in your non-dominant hand while threading a 4mm white glass pearl onto each.

3 Pass the end of one piece of memory wire through the loop of one of the faceted jet crystal rondelle bead units made in step 1. Pass the end of the other piece of memory wire through the loop at the other end of the same unit.

4 Thread two small pearls onto each piece of memory wire followed by another faceted jet crystal rondelle bead unit.

Tip

- Use bead stoppers to hold beads onto the piece of memory wire you are not working with.

- If you find the wire slippery when holding with your fingers, use chain-nosed pliers to pull and hold the beads tight.

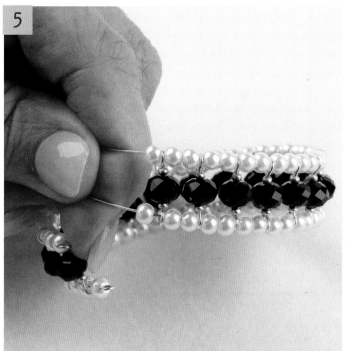

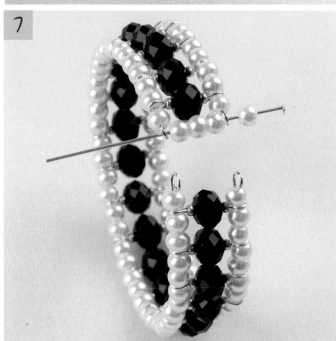

5 Repeat step 4 until all twenty-one crystal rondelle bead units have been strung onto the two pieces of memory wire with two pearls between. Finish with a single pearl.

6 Working with one piece of memory wire at a time, use memory wire shears to cut the excess wire, leaving approximately 8mm (¾in) or whatever length is needed to form a P-shaped loop (see page 12) to hold all the beads tightly in place.

7 To finish the ends, thread a small pearl on to a headpin. Pass the headpin through one P-shaped loop at the end of the bracelet. Add three small pearls to the same headpin then pass it through the second P-shaped loop. Make a wrapped loop as shown right (see page 14).

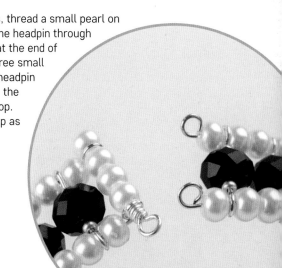

8 Use the instructions for making a wrapped loop on page 14 to make two dangles with a faceted jet crystal rondelle on each and two dangles with a 4mm white glass pearl on each (all dangles on the ball-end headpins). Be sure to attach the dangles to the wrapped loops formed in step 7 before wrapping the dangle loops! Attach one faceted jet crystal rondelle dangle and one small pearl dangle to each end of the cuff.

Design Inspiration

Evening in Paradise

It is so easy to make a wider memory wire cuff. All you do is add more beads when creating the eye pin bead units. This glorious confection of clear rondelles with foiled centres is embellished with real turquoise to bring out the cool blues and black faceted crystals to add a touch of mystery. Notice how bead units are staggered to give texture and interest.

BEADING WIRE

Beading wire (sometimes called tiger tail) is used for stringing beads and findings to make durable, flexible jewellery. Previously, stringing was done on thread, but the ease of use, durability and flexibility of beading wire have made it one of the most widely used materials today.

It is made up of multiple strands of fine stainless steel wire, twisted together and covered with a nylon coating.

It is available in different colours, diameters and break strengths. The most used is seven-strand but it can come with up to forty-nine strands. Surprisingly, the more strands, the more flexible and fluid the beading wire.

Tips for use

- *Unless floating beads, ensure all gaps between beads are removed so that no wire shows before crimping.*

- *Don't pull or stretch the wire too tight before crimping or the movement of the necklace will be stiff.*

- *It can be hard to remove or replace a squashed crimp bead without damaging the beading wire.*

- *Always use a new crimp bead even if you successfully remove an already squashed one, to ensure durability and strength.*

- *To ensure a necklace is the correct length, place one clasp end at the middle of the back of the neck and see where the beads come in the front. Add or subtract beads as required.*

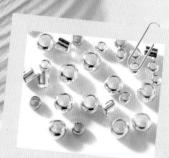

Crimp beads

Crimps or crimp beads are beads or tubes made of soft metal that hold when flattened. They come in different sizes and metal finishes. They are used for attaching clasps or beads to beading wire. They can also be used for floating beads on wire, thread or certain chains.

TOOLS

Memory wire shears   Round-nosed pliers   Chain-nosed pliers   Flush cutters

PRETTY IN PINK NECKLACE

Satin smooth pearls draw attention to the contrast of faceted opalescent pink and bright orchid crystals. The sparkling crystals in the diamante rondelle spacers add a finishing touch to this simple but beautiful necklace.

What you learn

- How to use crimp beads
- How to use bead tips/calottes
- How to make a single-strand design

MATERIALS

30 6 x 8mm pale pink opalescent faceted crystal rondelles

10 6 x 8mm AB translucent orchid faceted crystal rondelles

1 10mm ivory glass pearl

6 8mm ivory glass pearls

12 6mm ivory glass pearls

24 6mm diamante rondelle spacers

14 8mm diamante rondelle spacers

1m (39½in) silver colour beading wire/ tiger tail

2 silver-plated bead tips/calottes

2 2mm silver-plated crimp beads

1 silver-plated lobster clasp

1 9mm silver-plated jump ring

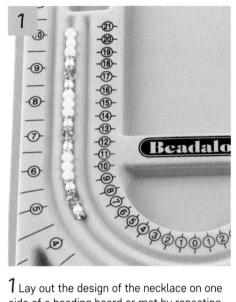

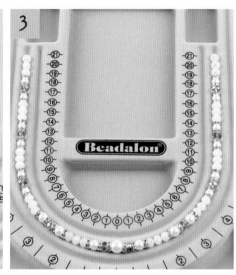

1 Lay out the design of the necklace on one side of a beading board or mat by repeating the following sequence three times, starting at the top left:
• 3 pale pink opalescent faceted crystal rondelles
• 6mm diamante rondelle spacer
• 6mm ivory glass pearl
• 6mm diamante rondelle spacer
• Orchid faceted crystal rondelle
• 6mm diamante rondelle spacer
• 6mm ivory glass pearl
• 6mm diamante rondelle spacer

2 Add the following sequence:
• 3 pale pink opalescent faceted crystal rondelles
• 8mm diamante rondelle spacer
• 8mm ivory glass pearl
• 8mm diamante rondelle spacer
• Orchid faceted crystal rondelle
• 8mm diamante rondelle spacer
• 8mm ivory glass pearl
• 8mm diamante rondelle spacer
• 3 pale pink opalescent faceted crystal rondelles
• 8mm diamante rondelle spacer
• 8mm ivory glass pearl
• 8mm diamante rondelle spacer
• Orchid faceted crystal rondelle
• 8mm diamante rondelle spacer

3 Repeat steps 1 and 2 from the top of the second (right) side. Add a 10mm ivory glass pearl where the two ends meet at the bottom. Set aside.

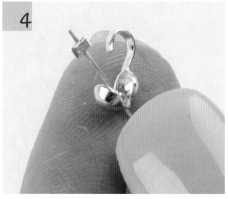

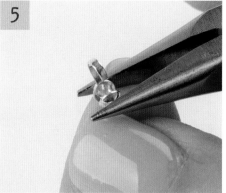

4 With chain-nosed pliers, flatten a crimp bead 2–3mm (1/8in) from one end of the beading wire/tiger tail. Thread the other end of the wire through a bead tip/calotte, going from the inside to the outside of the cup.

5 Pull the flattened crimp into the bead tip/calotte and, with chain-nosed pliers, gently close the cup over the crimp.

6 Starting at the open end, string beads on to beading wire as arranged in steps 1–3. Continue by threading the beading wire through a second calotte, this time from the outside to the inside of the cup. Add a crimp bead.

7 With chain-nosed pliers, pull the beading wire on the other side of the crimp bead to remove any slack. Flatten the crimp bead as close to the hole in the bead tip/calotte as possible to ensure there is no wiggle room or gaps of beading wire showing.

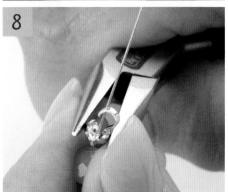

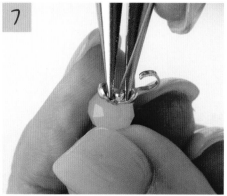

8 Gently close the cup over the flattened crimp.

9 With round-nosed pliers, close the hook of one bead tip/calotte around the lobster clasp. Close the hook of the other bead tip/calotte around the jump ring.

Tips

- Be sure the flattened crimp bead is secure on the beading wire/tiger tail. Pull and wiggle the wire to test whether it is held tightly in place.
- For added security, you can add a second crimp bead above the first one.

Copper Sparkle

The contrast of the sparkling crystals against satin glass pearls gives a delicate beauty to this tone-on-tone necklace. The simplicity in itself shouts out its elegance!

GOLDEN SATIN NECKLACE

Antique gold adds a vintage flavour to creamy glass pearls and glistening crystals on this upscale version of a pearl necklace.

What you learn

How to add dangles to single-strand beaded designs

1   Create a dangle by threading a small gold metal bead, a small AB crystal rondelle, a daisy spacer, a pearl, a second daisy spacer, a large AB crystal rondelle, a bead cap and a second small gold metal bead onto a headpin. Referring to the instructions on page 20, form a basic loop. Make a total of eleven dangles. Set aside.

2   With chain-nosed pliers, flatten a crimp bead 2–3mm (¹⁄₈in) from one end of the beading wire/tiger tail. Thread the other end through a bead tip/calotte, going from the inside to the outside of the cup. Pull the flattened crimp bead into the bead tip/calotte and with chain-nosed pliers, gently close the cup over the crimp bead (see steps 4 and 5 on page 32).

Tips

- Be sure the flattened crimp bead is secure on the beading wire/tiger tail. Pull and wiggle the wire to test it.
- For added security, you can add a second crimp bead above the first one.

3   Starting at one end, string beads in the following sequence, five times:

- Small gold metal bead
- Daisy spacer
- Two pearls
- Daisy spacer
- Small gold metal bead
- Daisy spacer
- Large AB crystal rondelle
- Daisy spacer

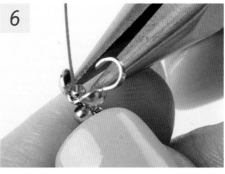

4 Continue with the following sequence, eleven times:

- Small gold metal bead
- Daisy spacer
- Pearl
- Dangle (made in step 1)
- Pearl
- Daisy spacer

5 Thread on a small metal bead, a daisy spacer, a large AB crystal rondelle and a daisy spacer, then repeat the sequence in step 3, four times. Finish with a small gold metal bead, a daisy spacer, two pearls, a daisy spacer and a final small gold metal bead.

6 Thread the beading wire through a second bead tip/calotte, this time from the outside to the inside of the cup. Add a crimp bead. With chain-nosed pliers, pull the beading wire on the other side of the crimp bead to remove any slack. Flatten the crimp bead as close to the hole in the bead tip/calotte as possible to ensure there are no gaps of beading wire showing.

7 Gently close the cup over the flattened crimp bead.

8 With round-nosed pliers, close the hook of one bead tip/calotte around the lobster clasp. Close the hook of the other bead tip/calotte around the jump ring.

Design inspiration

Classy Jet

Staggering the dangles is a marvellous twist to this
interesting and striking necklace. A touch of silver
brings out the classic beauty of the ever popular
faceted jet crystals.

MINTED NOODLE BRACELET

Taking advantage of the curves in these metal tubes called 'noodles', we have created a gorgeous bracelet that is stunning in its simplicity. Mint-green faceted crystals are interspersed with freshwater pearls with just a touch of bling from the diamante spacers.

What you learn

- How to use crimp beads with a wire guardian to attach a clasp
- How to include single and double-strand elements in the same piece

MATERIALS

6 3 x 4mm faceted mint-green opalescent crystal rondelles

2 4 x 6mm faceted mint-green opalescent crystal rondelles

2 6 x 8mm faceted mint-green opalescent crystal rondelles

4 4 x 6mm (approx.) button ivory freshwater pearls

1 8–10mm (approx.) ivory freshwater pearl

8 5mm diamante rondelle spacers

2 6mm diamante rondelle spacers

4 2 x 5mm antiqued silver-plated daisy spacers

4 38 x 2mm curved silver-plated metal tubes/noodles

½m (19¾in) silver-coloured beading wire/tiger tail

2 silver-plated wire guardians

2 silver-plated 2–3mm crimp beads

1 fancy silver-plated toggle clasp

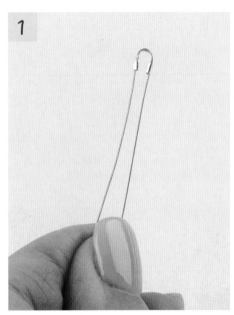

1 Thread the beading wire/tiger tail around a wire guardian, bringing the two ends of the wire together so that the wire guardian is resting in the centre fold of the wire.

2 Thread one end of the toggle clasp over the wire and onto the wire guardian so that it dangles from the middle of the wire guardian.

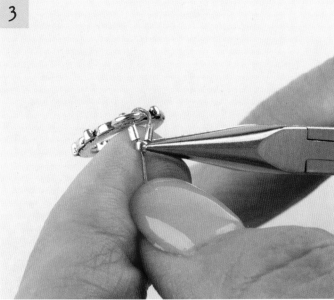

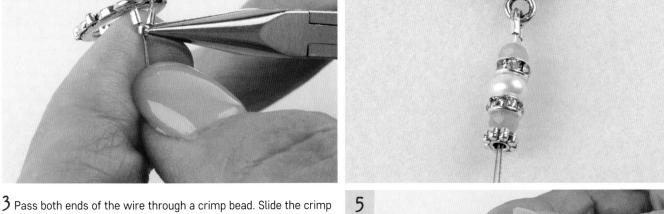

3 Pass both ends of the wire through a crimp bead. Slide the crimp bead next to the wire guardian and using chain-nosed pliers, flatten the crimp bead.

4 Pass both ends of the wire through the following sequence of beads:
- 3 x 4mm mint-green crystal rondelle
- 5mm diamante rondelle spacer
- 4 x 6mm freshwater pearl
- 5mm diamante rondelle spacer
- 3 x 4mm mint-green crystal rondelle
- 2 x 5mm daisy spacer

5 Split the beading wires. String a metal tube/noodle onto each wire.

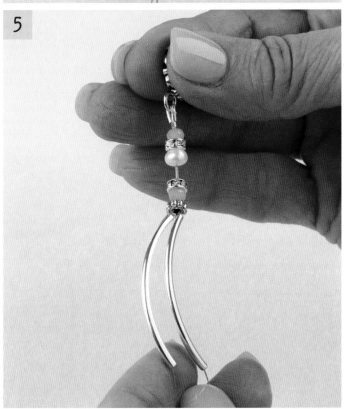

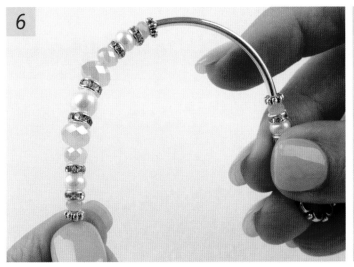

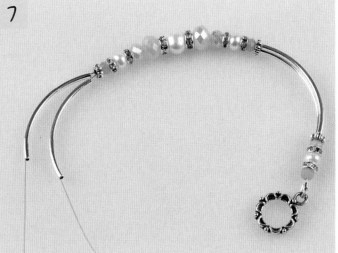

6 Bring the beading wires together and pass both through the following sequence of beads:

- 2 x 5mm daisy spacer
- 3 x 4mm mint-green crystal rondelle
- 5mm diamante rondelle spacer
- 4 x 6mm freshwater pearl
- 5mm diamante rondelle spacer
- 4 x 6mm mint-green crystal rondelle
- 6 x 8mm mint-green crystal rondelle
- 6mm diamante rondelle spacer
- 8-10mm freshwater pearl
- 6mm diamante rondelle spacer
- 6 x 8mm mint-green crystal rondelle
- 4 x 6mm mint-green crystal rondelle
- 5mm diamante rondelle spacer
- 4 x 6mm freshwater pearl
- 5mm diamante rondelle spacer
- 3 x 4mm mint-green crystal rondelle
- 2 x 5mm daisy spacer

7 Repeat step 5.

8 Bring the wire ends together and pass them through the same sequence of beads as in step 4, but in reverse.

9 Pass both wires through a crimp bead and around a wire guardian. Slip on the other side of the clasp so that it rests in the centre of the wire guardian.

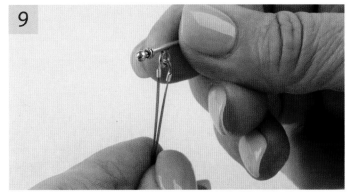

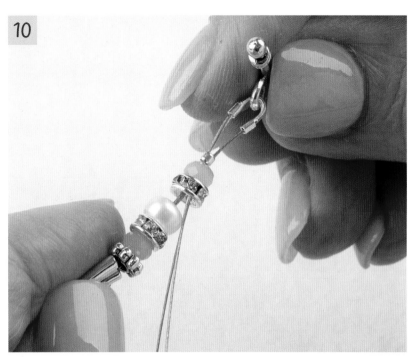

10 Pass both wires back through the crimp bead, the 3 x 4mm crystal rondelle and the 5mm diamante rondelle spacer.

11 Pull the wires tight to eliminate any gaps or exposed wire. With chain-nosed pliers, flatten the crimp bead. Trim away any excess beading wire using flush cutters.

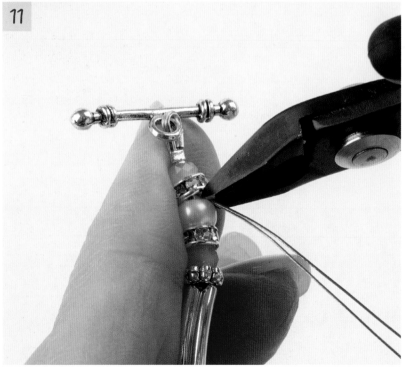

Design inspiration

Startdust Double Noodle Bracelet

Subtle shades of sage green, cream and tan glass chips combine to create the perfect backdrop to the stardust sparkle of the double noodle focus at the front of this attractive bracelet.

STRETCHY CORD

I have used both stretchy cord and what I call stretchy floss in these projects.

Stretchy cord stretches like an elastic band. Good quality cords keep their shape longer and are flexible, with an elegant drape. They are excellent for making stretch bracelets, power bracelets and hair bands. Stretchy cords usually come in clear or white but are also available in colours, the most popular being black, satin silver and satin gold. They come in various thicknesses: 0.5mm, 0.8mm and 1.0mm.

Stretchy floss is the name I give to a cord that has the appearance of dental floss, in that it is a cloudy white and looks flat rather than rounded. It is made up of several strands bonded together. It has a much softer drape than stretchy cord. Rings and bracelets made with stretchy floss tend to be more comfortable to wear. Stretchy floss comes in 0.3mm, 0.7mm and 1.0mm.

Tips for use

- The thicker the stretchy cord/floss, the stronger it is. Use the thicker ones with larger or heavier beads.
- When making a bracelet using numerous or heavy beads, use a double strand of stretchy cord/floss.
- When using a single strand of stretchy cord/floss, tie off with a double surgeon's knot (see page 48).
- When using a double strand, tie off with an overhand knot.
- Coil loops are less likely to slip off stretchy cord/floss.
- Using a split eye needle makes stringing beads onto stretchy cord/floss easier.
- Use clear nail varnish to seal and secure knots made in stretchy cord/floss.

TOOLS

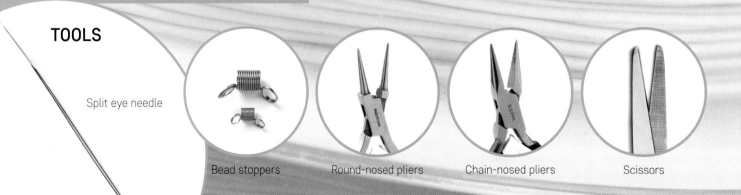

Split eye needle

Bead stoppers

Round-nosed pliers

Chain-nosed pliers

Scissors

GLITTER BALL RING

Stretchy cord or floss makes a perfect-fit ring. The contrast of the crystals on the glitter ball and diamante spacers with the sparkling jet crystal rondelles adds just the right touch of bling to this elegant ring.

What you learn

- How to use bead stoppers with stretchy floss
- How to tie a double surgeon's knot
- How to seal a knot with nail varnish
- How to conceal a knot

MATERIALS

8mm clear crystal glitter ball
2 5mm silver diamante rondelle spacers
15–18 3 x 4mm faceted jet crystal rondelles
20cm (8in) stretchy floss
Clear nail varnish

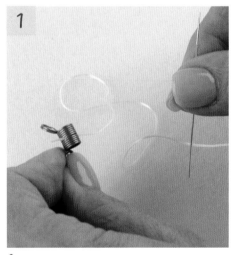

1 Thread about 3cm (1¼in) of the length of stretchy floss through the eye of a split eye needle. Place a bead stopper over the long cord end.

2 Pass the needle and thread through the glitter ball, one diamante rondelle spacer, then the fifteen to eighteen jet crystal rondelles and the second diamante rondelle spacer.

Rings made with stretchy cord or floss are comfortable to wear and get over a ring sizing problem, which is that if you make a ring big enough to go over the knuckle, it is then too loose and twists round, because the finger on the other side is slimmer. The glitter ball and diamante spacers give you sparkle and elegance as well as a perfect fit.

3

MAKING A DOUBLE SURGEON'S KNOT

a Cross the left end of the cord over the right end, and bring it round.

b Pass the left end of the cord over a second time, then pull.

c Cross the right end of the cord over the left end twice, as in steps a and b, and pull tightly.

d Now pull all four strands that are coming out of the knot tightly, until it catches. Pull the two on the left to the left and the two on the right to the right.

3 Remove the needle and tie a double surgeon's knot, as shown in the diagram above.

4 Re-thread the needle to the longer strand of floss and pass it back through the glitter ball.

5 Seal and secure the knot with clear nail varnish. Pull the long end of floss until the knot pops into the glitter ball. Allow to dry, then cut away the excess floss. Let the knot hide inside the glitter ball.

Design inspiration

Natural Stone and Floral Rings

These two perfect-fit rings were made in the same way. In the foreground Natural Stone Ring, vintage-style bead caps push together two rondelle-shaped beads of natural stone to create an attractive feature ring that is sure to draw attention. In the background Floral Ring, a delicate resin flower bead is surrounded by silver metallic crystal rondelles, creating an adorable ring that is fun to wear.

SEASHORE CRYSTAL CHA-CHA RING

Reflecting the colours of tropical seas, this cluster of translucent and frosted beads on a shimmering band of silver pairs up with the matching bracelet in the next chapter. The term 'cha-cha' refers to the fun pom-pom shape of the piece. While the placement of beads may appear random, in order to ensure that the design is balanced, string the beads on the stretchy cord in a repeating pattern.

What you learn

- How to make a coil loop
- How to cluster beads on stretchy floss

MATERIALS

1 6 x 8mm faceted AB crystal rondelle
2 4 x 6mm faceted light blue opalescent crystal rondelles
2 4 x 6mm faceted white opalescent crystal rondelles
4 4 x 6mm faceted aqua translucent crystal rondelles
4 4 x 6mm faceted silver metallic crystal rondelles
15–18 3 x 4mm faceted silver metallic crystal rondelles
13 silver-plated ball-end headpins
20cm (8in) stretchy floss
Clear nail varnish

MAKING A COIL LOOP

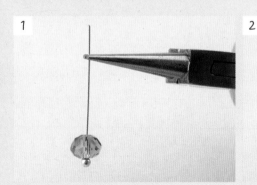

1 Thread the bead onto a headpin.

2 Use chain-nosed pliers to bend the wire at right angles, keeping the bend close to the bead.

3 Grab the end of the headpin about 5mm (¼in) from the tip of the round-nosed pliers. Roll the wire around one barrel of the pliers until the coil is tight against the bead.

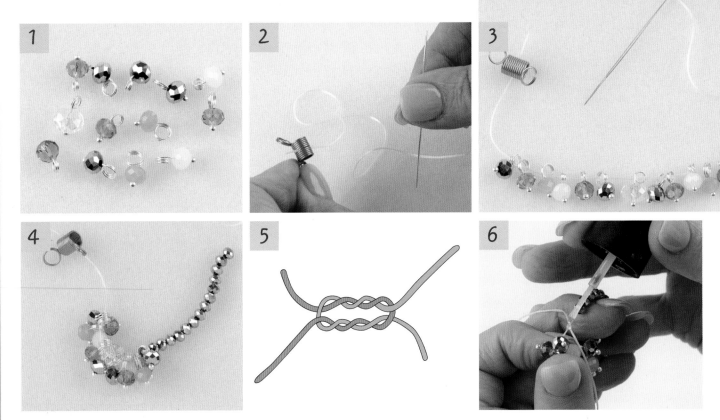

1 Thread each 4 x 6mm crystal rondelle bead (aqua, white, silver and light blue opalescent) and the 6 x 8mm AB crystal rondelle bead individually onto a ball-end headpin and form a coil loop (see page 50).

2 Thread about 3cm (1¼in) of the length of stretch floss through the eye of a split eye needle. Place a bead stopper over the long cord end.

3 Thread bead units onto the floss in the following sequence:
• 4 x 6mm silver crystal rondelle
• 4 x 6mm aqua translucent crystal rondelle
• 4 x 6mm light blue opalescent crystal rondelle
• 4 x 6mm white opalescent crystal rondelle
• 4 x 6mm aqua translucent crystal rondelle
• 4 x 6mm silver crystal rondelle
• 6 x 8mm AB crystal rondelle
• 4 x 6mm silver crystal rondelle
• 4 x 6mm aqua translucent crystal rondelle
• 4 x 6mm white opalescent crystal rondelle
• 4 x 6mm light blue opalescent crystal rondelle
• 4 x 6mm aqua translucent crystal rondelle
• 4 x 6mm silver crystal rondelle

4 Thread on fifteen to eighteen 3 x 4mm faceted silver crystal rondelles (the exact number is dependent on the size of ring required).

5 Remove the needle and tie a double surgeon's knot (see page 48).

6 Seal and secure the knot with clear nail varnish. Allow to dry, then cut away the excess floss using scissors. Let the knot hide between beads.

Design inspiration

Hot Pink Cha-Cha Ring

The bright neon shade of pink against a backdrop of jet black with sparkling silver highlights combine to create a touch of whimsy in this striking ring.

SEASHORE CRYSTAL CHA-CHA BRACELET

Bracelets made with stretchy cord or floss are popular because they are easy to slip on and off. Here shades of aqua and blue with touches of frosted opal and sparkling crystal cluster together to create a display of beaded opulence.

What you learn

✎ How to tie an overhand knot

MATERIALS

20 6 x 8mm faceted AB crystal rondelles
20 6 x 8mm faceted light blue opalescent crystal rondelles
40 4 x 6mm faceted white opalescent crystal rondelles
40 4 x 6mm faceted aqua translucent crystal rondelles
40 4 x 6mm faceted silver metallic crystal rondelles
120 silver-plated ball-end headpins
40 silver-plated decorative headpins
½m (19¾in) stretchy cord/floss

1 Thread each bead onto a headpin and form a coil loop (see page 50). Thread the smaller (4 x 6mm) beads on to ball-end headpins and the larger (6 x 8mm) beads onto decorative headpins.

2 Place the beaded units of the same colour and size together on your beading mat as shown.

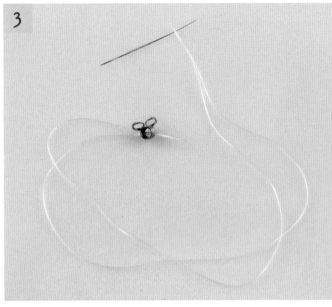

3 Thread the stretchy cord through the eye of a split eye needle, bringing the ends together for a double strand to give added strength. Place a bead stopper over the two cord ends.

4 Thread beads onto the cord in the following repeating sequence:
- 4 x 6mm aqua crystal rondelle
- 4 x 6mm silver crystal rondelle
- 4 x 6mm white opalescent crystal rondelle
- 6 x 8mm AB crystal rondelle
- 4 x 6mm aqua crystal rondelle
- 4 x 6mm silver crystal rondelle
- 4 x 6mm white opalescent crystal rondelle
- 6 x 8mm light blue opalescent crystal rondelle

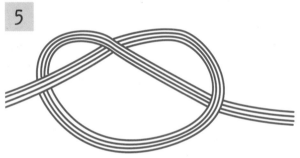

5 Cut the thread to remove the needle. Bring the four tails of cord together (two tails from each end) and tie an overhand knot, which is like tying the end of a balloon.

6 Seal and secure the knot with clear nail varnish. Allow to dry, then cut away the excess cord. Let the knot hide between beads.

Designer tip

For stunning results when designing a cha-cha bracelet, experiment with different sizes, shapes and colours of bead. Lighter-coloured beads can enhance bolder colours by making them stand out.

Design inspiration

Hot Pink Cha-Cha Bracelet

Brilliant pink adds a magnificent touch of colour to clusters
of sophisticated black and silver beads, creating a fabulous
display that can be worn at any time of the day or night.

CHAIN & JUMP RINGS

CHAIN

Jewellery chain has many aesthetic uses including circling the neck, wrists or ankles, and can also be used to hang pendants or decorative charms. It can be made from precious metals such as gold, silver and platinum, but less expensive plated base metals are more generally used for fashion jewellery.

Some of the more common types of chain include:

• Trace-links: uniform in breadth and thickness and usually simple and delicate
• Belcher: similar to trace, but the chain link is wider than its thickness and though often round, can also vary in shape
• Curb-links interlock when laid flat and have the largest variety of widths
• Rolo-links are usually identical and round and join in a simple alternating sequence
• Rope creates the effect of two strands twisted together
• Snake: very tight links with a round or square cross section
• Fancy: any metal shapes that can be joined together to create a chain (circular disc links, hearts, stars, etc.)

See page 74 for examples.

Tips for use

• To get the length of chain required, you can cut links with wire cutters (although some chains are too thick) or you can open the links by holding each side where the chain link joins with chain-nosed pliers and twisting.
• If cutting the chain, always hold both ends or position so that the loose end will not become a potential hazard to yourself or others. Place a hand or finger over where you are cutting or cut under a beading mat or inside a bag.
• When cutting wire, safety glasses are recommended.
• When choosing chain, consider the design uses and the weight of bead/s to determine its suitability.

Designer tips

• Create a chain bracelet, necklace or anklet by adding a clasp to chain.
• Add length to a piece by adding an extender chain to one end of the clasp, decorated with a bead or charm. The wearer can then change the length.
• Mixing different metallic finishes can add variety and interest as well as brightening up some colours.
• Chain with bead charms can be added to stretchy cord to create the popular chain links look.

TOOLS

Round-nosed pliers

Chain-nosed pliers

Bent-nosed pliers

Flush cutters

JUMP RINGS

Jump rings are usually circles, although they can be oval, square, triangular and other shapes. They are available in varying thicknesses with a join which allows the two sides to be opened and closed. They are made by wrapping wire around a mandrel to make a coil which is then cut to make individual rings. For a clean, uniform cut, chain maille artists (see opposite) prefer saw-cut jump rings. Jump rings can come in all kinds of materials but the most common are gold or gold-plated, silver or silver-plated, aluminium, brass, stainless steel, copper and titanium.

JUMP RING TERMINOLOGY

Gauge This is the thickness of the wire the jump ring is made from. The chart below gives the gauge and the thickness in inches and millimetres.

GAUGE	THICKNESS IN INCHES	THICKNESS IN MM
12	0.0808	2.05
13	0.0720	1.83
14	0.0641	1.63
15	0.0571	1.45
16	0.0508	1.29
17	0.0453	1.15
18	0.0403	1.02
19	0.0359	0.91
20	0.0320	0.81
21	0.0285	0.72
22	0.0254	0.65
23	0.0226	0.57
24	0.0201	0.51
25	0.0179	0.45
26	0.0159	0.40

Inner diameter This is a little bit larger than the outer diameter of the mandrel used to create the jump rings. The exact measurement depends on how much spring there is in the wire when it comes off the mandrel.

Outer diameter Twice the gauge plus the inner diameter.

Kerf The gap where jump rings are cut.

Jump ring tips

- To open a jump ring, grab each side of the join with chain-nosed pliers and twist so one side goes back and the other comes forward.

- To close a jump ring, twist each side of the join back into place, pushing a little past the point at which edges align, then twist back to align. This will help to break the spring of the wire.

- To ensure a tight, close fit of the cut edges of the jump ring, wiggle back and forth while pushing with inward pressure to close the gap (you will feel the edges rub together).

- Never open jump rings by pulling the ends apart outwards – this damages the shape. See page 66 for a diagram of the right way to open jump rings.

CHAIN MAILLE

While the most common use of jump rings is to attach two or more components together, they are also used to weave pieces, including jewellery, in a technique often referred to as chain maille.

Historically, chain maille goes back as far as Moses (1450 BC) and David and Goliath (1020 BC) while the earliest examples date from the 5th and 6th centuries BC. Chain maille was used by the Ancient Greeks and by the Roman military, and it is shown in the Bayeaux Tapestry. The use of chain maille during combat was phased out when hardened steel was invented and plate mail became a better protector.

Chain maille is still used as a protective shield today by butchers, in leather gloves, and shark divers use it in suits and gloves.

Designer tips

- Keep a pair of chain-nosed pliers in each hand (or a pair of chain-nosed and a pair of bent-nosed pliers) and use them to pick up and weave jump rings.
- Having jump rings pre-opened or pre-closed can help with learning a new weave (it is easier not to lose your place when following instructions).
- Mixing metals can add interest and variety.
- Beads can be added for extra colour and texture.

Chain maille tips

- The inside surface of the pliers should be smooth to prevent marking the jump rings. Prepare pliers for making chain maille by running a finger over the insides and edges of the jaws. Remove any rough bits with a soft cloth or fine grade sandpaper.
- The quality of the finished chain maille piece depends on seamlessly closed jump rings. Rough edges or gaps between the ends can ruin the look of the finished piece.
- Approaching the chain maille weave from the front and weaving away from you gives better control and a clearer view.

SWEETHEART CHARM BRACELET

This precious bracelet combines the sparkle of faceted crystals in shades of pink with the richness of satin freshwater pearls. These are embellished with silver hearts in different shapes and sizes to give an opulent yet whimsical appeal.

What you learn

✎ How to make a bracelet from ready-made chain
✎ How to cluster beads and charms on chain
✎ Practise wrapped loops

MATERIALS

18cm (7in) fancy twisted wire look silver chain, 10 x 12mm (³⁄₈ x ½in) oval links

1 oval silver-plated toggle clasp, 20 x 12mm (¾ x ½in) oval link

4 14mm (½in) silver-plated, open-centred heart charms

3 14mm (½in) antiqued silver-plated filigree heart charms

3 15mm (⁵⁄₈in) brushed silver-plated heart charms

11 6mm (¼in) antiqued silver-plated heart charms

11 6mm (¼in) AB round faceted crystal beads

11 6–8mm freshwater pearls

11 4 x 6mm pale pink faceted crystal rondelles

11 4 x 6mm pink opalescent faceted crystal rondelles

11 6 x 8mm silver faceted crystal rondelles

11 6mm rose faceted crystal bicone beads

9 2.4mm silver-plated round metal spacer beads

15 silver-plated headpins

61 silver-plated ball-end headpins

80 6 x 1mm silver-plated jump rings

1 Either cut the chain or open a link to get the desired length for the bracelet, taking into account the size of the clasp. Using chain-nosed pliers, attach each end of the clasp to an end of the chain with a jump ring or two.

2

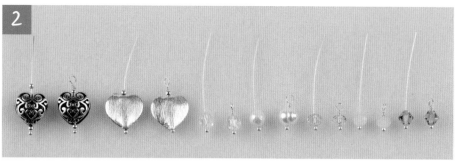

Copper and Jet Charm Bracelet

The copper tones of goldstone embellished with decorative bead caps enhance a dramatic setting of jet crystals. Faceted lentil-shaped crystals in shades of amber add sparkle to this stunning colour combination.

3

2 Make three wrapped loop units (see page 14) from a ball-end headpin threaded through a metal spacer bead, the 14mm (½in) antiqued filigree heart charm and another metal spacer bead. Repeat with the three brushed silver heart charms, each with a metal spacer bead at the top. Repeat with the eleven AB round faceted crystal rondelles, the eleven freshwater pearls, the eleven pale pink faceted crystal rondelles, the eleven pink opalescent faceted crystal rondelles and the eleven rose faceted crystal bicone beads. Set aside.

3 Make a wrapped loop (see page 14) from a headpin threaded through the four 14mm (½in) open-centred heart charms. Then make eleven wrapped loop bead units from the small 6mm (¼in) heart followed by a silver faceted crystal rondelle. Set aside.

4 Attach the beads to the chain links in the following sequence:

4

- Link 1, left: Pink opalescent faceted crystal and freshwater pearl
- Link 1, right: Rose faceted crystal bicone, AB round faceted crystal, small heart charm with silver faceted crystal
- Link 2, left: Open-centred heart charm
- Link 2, right: Pale pink faceted crystal
- Link 3, left: Rose faceted crystal bicone, AB round faceted crystal, small heart charm with silver faceted crystal
- Link 3, right: Pink opalescent faceted crystal and freshwater pearl
- Link 4, left: Pale pink faceted crystal
- Link 4, right: Brushed silver heart charm
- Link 5: same as Link 1
- Link 6, left: Antiqued filigree heart charm
- Link 6, right: Pale pink faceted crystal
- Link 7: Same as Link 3
- Link 8, left: Pale pink faceted crystal
- Link 8, right: Open-centred heart charm

- Link 9: Same as Link 1
- Link 10, left: Brushed silver heart charm
- Link 10, right: Pale pink faceted crystal
- Link 11, left: Same as Link 3
- Link 12, left: Pale pink faceted crystal
- Link 12, right: Antiqued filigree heart charm
- Link 13: Same as Link 1
- Link 14: Same as Link 2
- Link 15: Same as Link 3
- Link 16: Same as Link 4
- Link 17: Same as Link 1
- Link 18: Same as Link 6
- Link 19: Same as Link 3
- Link 20: Same as Link 8
- Link 21: Same as Link 1

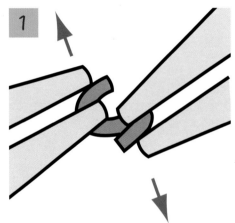

TWO-ON-TWO CHAIN MAILLE BRACELET

This elegant bracelet is one of the easiest chain maille weaves, yet looks so sophisticated, with a structured drape. With a few more jump rings, the bracelet can easily be widened by adding a third or fourth strand. It can also be embellished with beads to add colour and interest.

MATERIALS
224 silver-plated 6 x 1mm jump rings
1 silver-plated toggle clasp

What you learn

- How to open and properly close jump rings
- How to create double-strand chain maille from jump rings
- How to weave patterns using jump rings

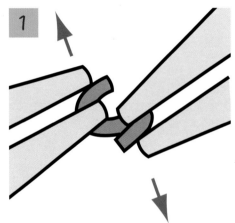

1 Open and properly close (see Jump ring tips, page 60) eighty-eight jump rings using two pairs of chain-nosed pliers.

2 Take one open jump ring and attach two closed jump rings to one end of the clasp. Take a second open jump ring and go around the same two closed jump rings and the clasp. This gives you the beginning of the first chain, which begins with the clasp followed by two sets of two jump rings.

3 Take one open jump ring and attach two closed jump rings to the last set of two jump rings of the first chain. Take a second open jump ring and go around the same two closed jump rings, making a total of four sets of two jump rings hanging from the clasp. Continue until forty-four open and forty-four closed jump rings are used (or as many as are needed to create the desired length, with an allowance for the clasp).

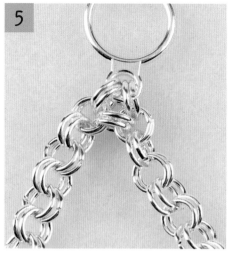

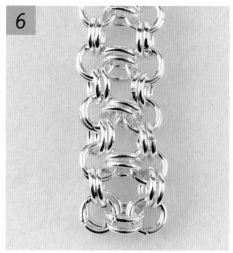

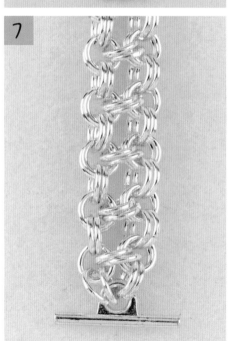

4 Repeat steps 1–3 to make a second identical chain next to the first one, using the same number of open and closed jump rings.

5 Open all remaining jump rings (or two jump rings for every other set of links in the two chains). Skip the first set of jump rings (the ones attached to the clasp) and join the two chains together with two jump rings around the two sets of jump rings that are lying flat on the surface.

6 Repeat step 5 until the two chains are joined along their length and the last two sets of jump rings from each chain are flat.

7 With the final four open jump rings, attach each chain to the other end of the clasp.

Design inspiration

From back to front:

Adding a third (or even fourth) strand of two-on-two jump rings increases the width and the elegance of this striking bracelet.

Beads threaded onto headpins with a basic loop can be attached directly to a triple-strand two-on-two bracelet, as in the middle bracelet in shades of shimmering blue and aqua. Simply twist the headpin loop open, slip over a jump ring or jump rings and close the loop. Placement can be random or structured.

Beads add colour and interest and can easily be added to the gaps between the sets of jump rings on this double-strand bracelet using beading wire (tiger tail) which is attached at each end using crimp beads.

SHAGGY LOOP CHAIN MAILLE BRACELET

Shaggy loop is a chain maille technique in which extra rings are added to each ring in a two-in-one chain. In this bracelet, the free-flowing movement of jump rings in varying sizes and textures is stunningly feminine. There is an option to add beads for an even more sumptuous effect.

What you learn

✎ How to weave more elaborate patterns using jump ring clusters
✎ How to attach beads to chain maille

MATERIALS

52 silver-plated 6 x 1mm jump rings
48 8mm silver-plated twisted wire jump rings
72 9 x 1.5mm silver-plated jump rings
1 silver-plated toggle clasp

1 Open twenty-four large and four small jump rings, following the diagram on page 66. Continue by ensuring that forty-eight large, forty-eight twisted and forty-eight small jump rings are properly closed. Make a jump ring cluster by threading two small, two twisted wire and two large jump rings onto a large open jump ring. Close the jump ring

2 Make another jump ring cluster and add it to the previous cluster, arranging it so there is a small, a twisted wire and a large jump ring on either side of the main ring.

3 Repeat, using all twenty-four large open jump rings as main rings (see step 2) or until the chain is the desired length, taking into account the size of the clasp.

4 Use two small jump rings to attach each end of the clasp to an end of the chain.

5 To add beads, thread each bead onto a headpin and form a basic loop as shown on page 20. Use a small jump ring to attach bead units to the large jump ring chain at the core of the bracelet, at regular intervals.

Shaggy Loop with Beads

Turn a beautiful bracelet into a gorgeous explosion of colour by adding
glass pearls in coordinating colours and faceted crystals to bling it up.

Jewellery Jargon Buster

AB (AURORA BOREALIS)

A steam treatment for beads which creates a shimmering effect in rainbow colours.

BALL-END HEADPIN

A length of wire with a decorative round ball end, which holds a bead on the wire while a loop is formed above it, to attach the bead to a jewellery piece. See page 14 for making a wrapped loop or page 20 for making a basic loop.

BEAD CAPS

These are usually metal. They are used to enhance a bead or stone, to go between the end of a string of beads and the clasp, to protect precious beads from rubbing against each other or to hide discolouration or blemishes on beads.

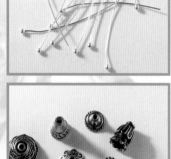

BEAD TIP/CALOTTE

A small metal finding which resembles a clam shell with a hook at the end. The cup closes over a knot and/or a crimp bead to conceal and protect the end while giving a professional finish. The hook is used to attach the clasp when finishing a jewellery piece.

BEADING WIRE/TIGER TAIL

Multiple strands of fine stainless steel wire, tightly twisted together and covered with a nylon coating. Used for stringing and/or floating beads and findings to create durable and flexible pieces.

BICONE BEADS

Glass beads shaped like two faceted cones joined together at their base.

CALOTTE

see Bead tip

CHAIN

A series of linked metal rings in a variety of ring shapes and sizes.

- Cable

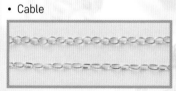

- Rope

- Trace links

- Rolo links

- Curb links

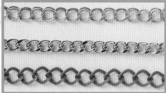

CHAIN MAILLE

Armour or jewellery made by connecting metal rings to one another. Chain maille jewellery is made by linking jump rings in various patterns and weaves.

CHARMS

Decorative pendants, trinkets or beads that may signify something important to the wearer. Used to decorate jewellery including earrings, bracelets and necklaces.

CHIPS

Irregular stone chippings, usually from semi-precious stones such as amethyst, aquamarine, quartz, jasper, onyx and more.

CLASP

A device or fastener used for attaching or holding the ends of jewellery together.

A lobster clasp is in the shape of a lobster claw. It is held closed by a spring that is operated by a small lever. Also called a parrot clasp or a trigger clasp.

A toggle clasp is made up of a bar and a ring with the bar fitting through the ring to fasten the clasp. The beads next to the bar must be small enough to pull through the ring (or a few jump rings or links of chain can be added to the bar end).

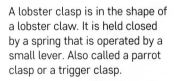

CRIMP BEADS

Small beads made of soft metal that hold components in place when flattened with pliers. Used to secure wire ends when attaching clasps or beads to beading wire. Also used to float beads on wire or certain chains.

CRYSTAL RONDELLES

Faceted crystal beads that have a 'squashed' rounded shape. Also known as faceted crystal rondelles, faceted crystal donuts and squashed round crystals.

CURVED METAL TUBES

see Noodles, page 77

DAISY SPACERS

Decorative flat spacer beads in the shape of a daisy (sometimes called snowflake spacers).

DIAMANTE RONDELLE SPACERS

Also called crystal rondelle spacers. These look like tyre hubcaps with diamante stones decorating the rim. They are used between beads to add interest and sparkle.

EARRING WIRES

Wire findings for making earrings. They have a wrapped loop at one end onto which you can attach beaded units.

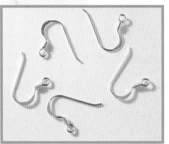

EXTENDER CHAIN

A short length of fine chain, often with a filial or bead ending that allows the option of adding length to a necklace or bracelet.

EYE PIN

A length of wire with a pre-formed loop end used to link two things together.

FACETED CRYSTAL RONDELLES

see crystal rondelles, page 75

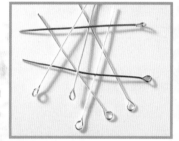

FRESHWATER PEARLS

These are produced in freshwater mussels which create a pearl sac to seal off an irritant, usually introduced by human intervention.

GLASS PEARLS

These are made to imitate pearls, with a glass base that is then dipped in a coating to create colour and lustre.

GLASS RONDELLES

Small flat discs of glass with colour coatings and a hole for stringing.

GLITTER BALLS

Clay beads with crystal pave – an all-over sparkling surface. There are different grades depending on the quality of the crystals, with Czech crystals at the high end and acrylic 'glass' at the opposite end.

HEADPIN

A length of wire which can be ball-end (see top, right) flat or decorative (right, bottom). Flat ones have a flat head like a nail. The end holds a bead on the wire while a loop is formed at the other end and used to attach beads to a jewellery piece.

JUMP RINGS

Circles of wire, available in varying thicknesses with a join allowing the ring to be opened and closed. Used to attach two components. Available in different shapes with round and oval being the most popular.

MEMORY WIRE

Spring-tempered wire with a hard temper that holds a coiled shape. It comes in necklace, bracelet and ring sizes and is used for designs that need to keep their shape.

METAL SPACER BEADS

Beads made of plated precious or base metal. They come in many different shapes and sizes and are used to separate patterns on beaded jewellery.

NOODLES/CURVED METAL TUBES

Hollow metal tubes in a macaroni shape. They come in different metals, lengths, diameters and angles of bend. They can be used as spacers on threads, cords or wire.

NUGGETS

Irregular-shaped gemstones or semi-precious beads that are smoothed to remove sharp edges and have a hole or holes for stringing. Also known as semi-precious chips. They can also be glass or acrylic.

RESIN FLOWER BEADS

Resin moulded into various flower shapes, sizes and colours. They often come as flat-backs without holes for stringing.

SEED BEADS

Small beads made from long pipes of glass, often used for weaving jewellery designs, for stringing or as spacer beads. The most popular sizes start at 15°, which is the smallest, up to 6°, which are called pony beads.

SEMI-PRECIOUS CHIPS

SHELL RONDELLES

Small flat discs made of shell with a hole for stringing.

STARDUST BEADS

Metal beads with a textured coating that glistens and come in a variety of colours and sizes to add sparkle to jewellery designs.

STRETCHY CORD/FLOSS

Stringing material that is stretchy and comes in a variety of strengths and colours. It can be used to make bracelets and rings that are easy to slip on and off. Stretchy floss (also called Elonga) is made up of several individual stretchy strands bonded together for superior elastic properties, giving a soft, silky drape to jewellery pieces.

WIRE GUARDIANS

Horseshoe-shaped metal tubes that are open at the curve and used to protect wires and threads in places where they get more wear and tear. They give a professional look to jewellery endings.

Tools

BEAD STOPPER

A gadget made up of tightly coiled metal wire that is used to secure the end of a project in progress, keeping beads, wire or components in position.

BENT-NOSED PLIERS

Similar to chain-nosed pliers but with curved jaws. Half the length of the jaws is bent at an angle away from the centre of the pliers. These are used to reach into tight places, bend wire, open and close jump rings, close bead tips/calottes and attach clasps. The bent jaws allow access without blocking vision.

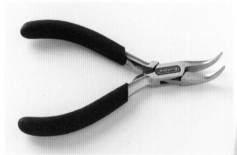

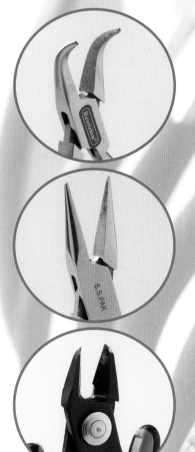

CHAIN-NOSED PLIERS

These have jaws that are flat on the inside and rounded on the outside. They are used to hold findings, components, wire, cords, etc. They are good for getting into tight spaces where fingers can't reach and can hold components more securely than fingers. When working with wire, make sure the insides of the jaws are smooth, as ridged or textured jaws will mark the wire.

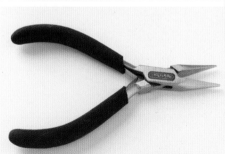

FLUSH CUTTERS

The jaws of flush cutters have a flat side and a beveled side. They are used to make smooth, flat, neat cuts in wire. The flat side gives a straight cut and the bevelled side gives a V-shaped cut.

MEMORY WIRE FINISHING PLIERS

The barrels are one small rod and one large rod. This allows for loops of a consistent size. Cone-shaped round-nosed pliers can slip when you are trying to form a loop from the hardened steel of memory wire, but memory wire finishing pliers have straight, cylindrical barrels which eliminate this and make it easier to form loops.

MEMORY WIRE SHEARS

These specialised heavy-duty cutters are used particularly for cutting memory wire (spring tempered wire) and heavy gauged wire.

REAMER

A round, tapered file used to clear, smooth or enlarge the inside of the bead hole. Also useful when tying knots and a useful aid when weaving chain maille. The one shown on the left is battery operated.

ROUND-NOSED PLIERS

Both jaws are tapered cones used for creating loops as well as bending and shaping wire. Having tapered cones for barrels allows different sizes of loop to be formed according to what is required. Most commonly used to create loops on eye pins or headpins that are used for attaching beads and components.

SPLIT EYE NEEDLE

This has an eye that spans almost the whole length of the needle and makes it easy to thread most sizes of thread and cord. It is incredibly flexible and perfect for bead projects.

Index